I0464435

Gamification - engage customers in your business!

The hottest marketing trend in 2014

Written by Benjamin Borowski

Based on Pawel Tkaczyk Gamification Training

CONTENTS

Introduction

The Harvard Business Review named gamification one of the largest trends in marketing. From that time, an increasing number of enterprises decide to turn to gamification to boost their business. It's a trend you should look at for marketing as well as educational applications. I'm going to tell you about what gamification is and isn't. I'm going to use an illustration to give you a run-through of this concept.

Imagine you get into a prototype car that asks you right away to submit your Facebook login and password. The vehicle has onboard web connectivity. Why do you need to feed your Facebook credentials to it? If you do, the car will personalize. It can adjust your seat to your liking, find and play your favorite radio stations and set the rear-view mirror just like you like it.

Let's assume you're using a new GPS app. You enter a waypoint: your route is going to be from New York to Baltimore. You can run on a freeway on your trip for about 140 miles. The car will go: 140 miles on a freeway. Last week, your brother-in-law Mark used 2.2 gallons on the same trip. Wanna play? Wouldn't you?

What the gamification is?

Feel the zeal

Gamification is about adding fun to the tasks and activities that aren't entertaining normally.

There is a multitude of stuff you know on a cerebral, intellectual level that you must do, but simply can't muster up the energy or don't have the zeal. A case in point: quitting smoking. You know that cigarettes are bad for you but your brain will be less than happy about a withdrawal. The same goes for saving up on gas. Very often you realize well you need to improve your fuel economy, especially as gas pump charges make you reach for a tissue or Valium. Some studies show that driving economically can save you up to 20% on fuel consumption. This means you get one free refuel out of five. Now, what economy driving really is? It's slow and boring. You can't speed up, can't accelerate and stop rapidly and so on. Every day, you keep promising that you're going to start paying attention to your gas mileage. And every day, you have to get to work on time, drive kids to school or preschool, get somewhere on time. To add to that, there's that guy at red lights who taunts you with a loud vroom of the engine… Your promise was good while it lasted.

You know where it hopped off to? To a place where all motivation goes to die. There's a day we all choose as the jumping off point for saving, motivating, dieting and so on. That day is tomorrow. We keep telling ourselves, "Right, I didn't make it this time, but I'll start over tomorrow." And why do we keep failing? Essentially, we fail because saving fuel is not fun. We need an extra mechanism that will turn all these tedious doings—saving on fuel, healthy eating and so on—into entertainment. The same applies to education.

Bikini potatoes

I wanted to talk about education and learning at a greater length as they are the background from which many gamification mechanisms come. Learning is dull by definition. Take a look at the balls behind me. If I asked you which of them is cramming for a test, the answer is obvious. The sad ball.

Learning as such is dull. It's not fun. But are you sure? Generally, in-school learning is hardly ever a pleasure but there can be many different faces to education. You can pick up certain skills and knowledge in passing, unbeknownst even to yourself. To explain this, we'll go a couple centuries back to the times of Frederick the Great.

Frederick the Great was King of Prussia, a very clever monarch who was at constant war with a bunch of countries. Now, how do you wage war? Wars need armies. Napoleon Bonaparte used to say that an army marches on its stomach. To keep an army, you need to feed your soldiers. The soldiers in the times of Frederick ate two staple foods. The first was meat. Meat was costly. To have pork for dinner, you'd first have to raise a pig, muck it out, fill the manger and so on.

The other army staple food was grains. The soldiers munched on bread, buns, flatbread. Meat and bread were the two basic victuals they ate. The problem with this fare was that first, meat could run out quickly, and second, if a plague of insects destroyed crops, soldiers would be left with nothing.

You can't come up with good plans for a war if you are not sure if you can feed your army. Frederick had an idea. There was one ingredient he got from an Italian court that he wanted to include into his soldiers' food rations. He wanted his soldiers to eat potatoes.

They held back on potatoes for two reasons. First, they looked vile. Second, you need to understand what a Prussian army soldier ate back in Frederick's time. He ate meat—a noble foodstuff served at courts—and bread, which also was dirt-free. So when the king's order was, "Dude, from now on you will eat the tubers, grub them, scrape them clean, and fight your pig to get them." They didn't really consider potatoes fit for humans.

Now, what could Frederick do to make his soldiers eat potatoes? He was king, he could use his authority and say, "You will eat them." But Frederick was a notch above this. He was a smart king. He knew that while this would get the results and the soldiers would begin to eat potatoes, the morale of his army, a basic element of a battle, wouldn't be on par. What he really had to do is to make his soldiers want to eat potatoes. So what did he do? Think, what he could have done? He could've made potatoes look fancier. He could've grown a concept potato targeted at soldiers. A sutleress potato. This would be hard logistically.

13

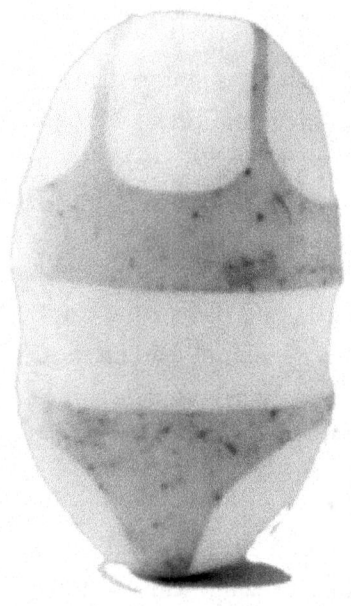

Just think about a second army of people cutting up potatoes in little bikinis. So what did Frederick do? He had a castle where he told his domestics to plow some beds and sow potato seeds in it. More than that, he had guards watching over the beds lest that some commoners pinch the royal kartoffeln. The royal potato could only be consumed by the king and the royal household. That was the official command the guards got, but off the record, they were told to take it easy with their job and take toilet and coffee breaks often and so on.

Now, if a Prussian peasant knew one thing, it was that if a crop is watched over, it's likely valuable and it might well be good to pinch it and grow. Over the next two years, East Prussia saw a rapid rise in underground—sic!—growing of the royal potato. When after this time Frederick approached his soldiers and told them to eat potatoes, their reaction wasn't, "But why?" Rather, they agreed, "Okay, great. Can I have the potatoes, Mom? Can I have the potatoes, Dad?" This is a classic example of a good teacher. A good teacher is someone who makes you learn stuff even when you don't even realize you're learning. This is what gamification is.

Gamification Karate Kid

It makes people gain knowledge, develop habits and new routines en passant. They will be drawn to your store, or start using your web service as a new addiction of sorts. Why does it have an addictive effect? Because it's fun. Most of the movies you like to watch that slip in a mentor trope are stories of picking up knowledge as you go. Remember Karate Kid, the first one, from the eighties? It was about a kid who wanted to learn karate. He found this old master, and the master said, "Sure, I will teach you, but go and paint this fence first." The kid paints the fence, then carries water, then does a lot of other stuff that isn't learning karate. And at some point he needs to use the karate skills. He must use the karate, and it turns out he's already learnt it.

The new 2010 Karate Kid with Jackie Chan tells the same story. A kid wants to learn karate, for one reason or another, and he achieves mastery by the way as well. That's gamification: people learn and become better at stuff that they would like to do on a purely intellectual level, like quitting smoking, losing weight, saving up on fuel and so on—the stuff they wouldn't be able to force themselves to do otherwise. But if you can persuade them, put the fun into it, so that they begin to get on with something in passing, they will really appreciate it.

The punch line is that gamification in marketing and education, as well as in HR and so on, is about gaining knowledge without learning because learning as such has become a term that is loaded with off-putting associations. We've come to associate work with something unpleasant. Work can be fun, too. Gamification is used in HR exactly for that: to motivate employees to work better. Talking of this rupture between work, learning and fun: where is the boundary? Where's the line between work, learning and fun? Is it real at all? I'm going to tell you a little story again.

Have you ever read The Adventures of Tom Sawyer? There's a chapter in this book where Tom's aunt tells him to whitewash a fence on a Sunday morning. For us, painting a fence is work. If Tom set about this task like we would do, he'd do it eventually, with a long face. At the end of the day his aunt would tell that he's a nice boy, and he'd be like, "Right. I worked like a hog all day, the Sunday is ruined." But Tom looked at this differently. Twain captured this in a really different way. Tom went ahead and started painting the fence with a lot of gusto. He went about it as if it was great fun. This is a scene Tom's buddies walk in on. They say, "Tom, your aunt ruined your Sunday because she told you to paint the fence," but Tom answers, "No, it's a lot of fun." They look at him in surprise and go, "If it's such a great fun, let us try!" Do you remember what Tom says to this? He says, "No, I won't let you try, unless you pay." By the end of the day, these guys do Tom's work, have fun doing it, and Tom cashes in on it as well. That's the real power of gamification. Turning an everyday activity into a play.

Work or fun?

I daresay work, learning and fun are not as mutually exclusive as you think. It's true that we feel there's a huge gap between the three. We can almost see it. But this wasn't the case always. Go back two thousand years back. Is being a serf a chore or a play? You'll say the former because you have an image of it that's rain or shine drudgery and a lord's whip.

But harvest days had a different face as well. Workers celebrated harvest with bonfires and frolicked around hay-stacks with young misses. They had great fun. Is sailing work or fun? The sailing life is again black skies but beer at taverns as well.

What about singing sea-shanties as they hurled a line or paddled? Is being a vassal, a lord, or a count work or fun as well? Granted, you could say 'it's just fun' to this. After all to feast on lamb shanks surrounded with a battery of domestics is anyone's dream. But when a lord calls, you need to take up a sword, leave for land and family, mount a nag and, basically, go meet your death. Doesn't seem like great fun at that point.

The Vikings. It's my favorite example. Being a Viking, is that work or fun?

There's a genius drawing that is as good a commentary on it as it gets. Two Vikings are having a chit-chat, and one says to the other, "What I like most about being a professional Viking is rape." You can't separate work and fun in a clear way. When did this division start to apply anyway? When did work and fun become detached from one another? Why is the boundary there at all?

The answer can be found in history. Vikings, vassals and peasants did not go to work. They didn't see any rift between the time they spent on working, learning and celebrating. Their life was a unity of the three. The rift appeared with the emergence of employment as we know it today. The Industrial Revolution and a rise of factories were the starting point of employment. Looking back at the thousands years of human history, it was only a wink ago, and it has changed our lives. No longer interweaving work, learning and fun, we had to switch over to separated blocks of time and place. I go to a factory for an 8-hour shift: that's work. Work I get paid for. The guy who pays cannot care less if I'm having fun or it's mind-numbing. I get my remuneration for the time I spent in the factory. I can then use the hard-won money to buy fun and pleasure outside the factory, which creates a further chasm.

Good gamer

I want to prove it to you that there is no discernible difference between the activities you do for work and the activities you do for fun. What Tom Sawyer did should clue you in on this a bit. Here's a contemporary example: IBM. This company hired Professor Leighton Reed to run an in-house recruiting session to find good candidates for managers inside the company rather than hire them from the outside. Leighton Reed could have approached this task in a standard way. He could've told IBM staff to take HR tests or had everyone gather around in a room and then said, "Alright, we'll do some personality testing, then some leadership testing, and a bunch of other tests. Based on the results, we'll pick candidates for managers." But they took a wildly different road. Before I tell you about this, I'm going to tell you about a spreadsheet. Think about an accountant who's making a living out of feeding budgets into a spreadsheet for 8 hours straight. When he gets home, he sits down, opens a spreadsheet and types data into it some more—for fun. You know what he's doing? He's playing World of Warcraft.

If you have lived under a rock for the past ten years, World of Warcraft is an MMORPG. I'll break this down for you: a Massively Multiplayer Online Role-Playing Game. Massively Multiplayer means that hundreds, tens of thousands or millions of players are gaming at the same time. World of Warcraft has now about 15 million paying players. They pay a monthly fee, 19 dollars, to play the game. Online means the entire game is played over the web. World of Warcraft is difficult.

While there are some tasks you can do as a newbie on your own, you won't complete many other things if you don't work as a team. You can do a bunch of stuff with other players, for example exchange and sell stuff. If you find and collect an item, you need to know if it's better to trade it right away or keep it for some time. This is what our accountant is calculating in the spreadsheet. He's got a special spreadsheet for keeping track of his items, tracks their auction prices, and checks if they should be sold already, if he'll make money on the transaction or not. It's an intricate issue.

Now, let's steer back to the IBM conference room. When Leighton Reed put all the engineers together in a room, he didn't ask them about their skills. He only asked one question: "Which of you is a WOW guild leader?" A guild is an in-game association of players. A guild leader is a player character who's been selected as the leader and who is in charge of managing the association. Research shows that controlling a guild in World of Warcraft takes more brainpower and skills than middle management in a corporation. A guild leader has to gather a team, organize people, and plan for a lot scenarios as some missions in WOW can only be completed in teams of more than ten people. You need to group the players, train them, plan a quest or raid, create a plan B and so on. WOW guild leaders are people who can make good managers at IBM. When Reed and his partners asked people what they had learnt in World of Warcraft, they reeled off a long list. They had learnt good communication skills, fostered persuasion, and so on. The same skills that are needed at work are required for playing. The only difference between working and playing is here. It's in your head.

Let's now go back to Fordism. An artificial chasm between work and playing emerged when people began to go to workplaces, when we were deprived of fun and choice. Fordism is illustrated well by this quote from Henry Ford, "Any customer can have a car painted any color that he wants so long as it is black." Why do I mention this if my primary topic is work and school? Because that's what production lines looked like in the past. That's what workplaces were like.

Today our workplaces for the most part also don't welcome our own contributions, don't make room for our own preferences and favorite items. You're working in an open plan workspace that only allows you to customize the picture you put on a desk, a photo of your family or a picture of your cat. This was the time when the modern industry and the modern idea of 'going to work' first took shape. And coincidentally, this was also the time when the modern educational system emerged, and 'going to school' became a reality.

Look at the difference between a production line at a factory and a classroom. The kids are standardized. They're all alike. A case in point: how are kids signed up for a class? Are their skills tested? No. They're sorted by their date of manufacture. A school is like a factory, like a factory production line. It's linear and doesn't offer alternatives, but you can't argue that this kid is exactly like that kid, or rather if he should be exactly like that other kid. If you let your child pass through an educational system, the only place they will be able to work after they graduate is a modern factory.

The modern production line is a regulated, homogeneous place.

Everything's set in the minutest detail. A good example of it is, say, McDonald's. Everything that takes place there is provided for in a manual. There's no room for customization. Meanwhile, the modern consumer—if we move on to marketing because this topic isn't just about education and includes modern purchase behavior as well—he wants to have access to all sorts of gizmos and gadgets that are personalized. If I buy a computer today, obviously I can choose its size, the color of the case and so on. I want a pink PC, or a green PC. If I go to a store to buy an iPod, one of the basic metrics I will choose is color. It's customization. I don't know if you've seen a kid who got his first Xbox. A ten-year-old or a twelve-year-old who gets his first Xbox, a video game console, will spend most of the time on customizing his avatar, making this character fit the idea in his head. Even if theoretically this isn't rewarding. What could be the reward of having an avatar have the same red hairdo? At a glance, it's pointless. But there has to be something it in. When we'll go into gamification, I'd like us to look into this concept. Is fun and work mutually exclusive? When I enter a workplace, do I need to switch off fun altogether? At school, do I need to be bored? No pain, no gain, the old saying goes. But is it really true?

Buy a product

Teamwork

Whenever I'm giving a talk on gamification I run a quick group test that we can't do now because we don't have direct contact. I split a group of 6, 10 or 12 into two or three teams and assign a simple task: Buy a product. What am I selling? This could be anything from a book, a bottle of water to a bag of salty sticks.

It's an auction that follows a different principle than usual. The rules are as follows: you bid on your own but win as a team. The goal is to win a bottle or a book for your team. All bidders call out their bids individually. The catch is that it's not the highest bid that wins an item, it's the second-highest bid that wins.

Team rules are straightforward: keep bidding, and the second-highest bid wins. What's crucial is to come up with an adequate strategy for the auction, because the standard bid up approach is just not applicable. If Team A bids 10 dollars and Team B outbids them with 11 dollars, which team wins? Keep in mind that it's the second-highest bid that wins, so the winning bid is 10 dollars even if Team B offers more.

What can you do as a team? One of the strategies you can try out is double overbidding. The first team bids 10, Team B gives 11 dollars, and just after that someone else from this team places a higher bid at 12 dollars: the item will only stay in this team then. Why am I talking about this? Try to arrange this non-standard auction in your office, among your friends. Split them into teams and see how much they are willing to fork out for your product under these circumstances. The punch line? People I make bid at my auctions use real cash to play.

I got a bid of 25 dollars for a book that costs 13. For snacks that are worth 1 dollar I got 10. That's how powerful gamification can be. When people warm up and start to really get into this, get the fun, you'll see that entertainment is just as big in the overall picture in the auction as wanting to buy a product.

Gamification inside the cars

Automobile manufacturers like Honda, Nissan or Ford have long experimented in using elements of gamification for their products. That's the Honda Insight. The 2010 model, a hybrid electric vehicle. People who drive this car save up to 20 per cent of fuel compared to folks who drive the same model but have disabled the Eco Assist system. What is Eco Assist about? Long story short, Eco Assist is in-car gamification. A bunch of Ford models incorporate a similar system. The Nissan Leaf took it to a whole new level. Just wait for it.

How does gamification go with the Honda Insight? Remember, the car has a built-in system that 'forces' you to save fuel. Mind you, I use force in inverted commas. The basic rule of all games is that they are played freely. You're not forced to do anything per se, however some clocks in your head are turned to a next level. What is this level?

Have you ever ridden an elephant? If you skipped on this pleasure, imagine a guy who's on top of a big grey elephant. But who is really on top in this relationship? The man or the elephant?

If you say man, it shows you haven't ever done it. If an elephant wants to go somewhere, carrot, stick or whip, it will. An elephant is a thick-skinned mammal. If it wants something, it gets it. If you say an elephant is on top in this relationship, you're right to a large extent. But this would make riding an elephant a pointless exercise.

If the elephant is completely free to go whichever way it desires, why mount it in the first place? It will not go where you want it to go after all. The truth however is that a rider is able to control the elephant a bit, for some time, by coaxing it to go where the rider wants it to be.

Why elephants and riders? Inside your head, inside the head of everyone in the world, there is an elephant and a rider. The rider is the rational part of your brain, the part that knows you need to economize your fuel consumption, the part that knows you should be cramming for a test, the part that knows you need to hold back on snacks in favor of health food. But there's also an elephant inside you, an instinct-driven creature that wants instant gratification. The elephant is as primitive as it gets. The banana peel is that it's also very strong.

Want to see how the rider and the elephant clash against each other? Imagine you're comfortably in bed and need to go to work. The clash between your inner rider and the elephant is always this: you need to egg on the elephant. Cheat it. Make it want the same thing the rider wants. At an intellectual level, you realize perfectly well you need to be up on time or your boss fires you, which then would mean you can't buy stuff to keep yourself and the elephant happy. But in the wee small hours of the morning, the elephant says, "Dude, give me five minutes. It's dark out there, it's cold, it's going to rain, no, it will hail today. Stay under the blanket."

So what do you do to take the elephant for a ride? In the evening the day before, when you're still governed by intellect rather than instinct, you put on an alarm clock. The elephant will wake up and tell you to stay in bed. So what have we, clever riders, done to deal with this? We've created the snooze button. When our elephant wakes up and smacks the clock off, we have predicted this would happen. Thankfully, because of the snooze button the clock will ring again in five minutes.

I know of more drastic solutions as well. There's a gizmo called Clocky. It's an alarm clock that blasts off the vilest of sounds in the morning and wheels away from you as you are desperately trying to catch it. You need to crawl out of bed, and that's what the rider wanted you to do all along—drag the elephant out of bed. Congrats, you just took the elephant for a ride.

An even more severe solution was thought up in Russia. A clock integrated with a paper shredder. In the evening you put a bill in and once it sounds off, the shredder begins to work. You wake up and see in your mind's eye how your twenty bucks or hundred bucks—depending on how badly you need to get up on time—is cut into strips. You don't generally put in rubles, because why would you?

This is a solution that works like a charm. You cheat your inner animal and do this using gamification. The elephant is really unwilling to do some stuff, but you con it, divert its attention and make it look the other way. The elephant begins to do what you want it to do by the way.

Let's go back to the Honda Insight. How do the rider and the elephant collaborate in this car? Just so you know, the rider and elephant metaphor was not developed by me. I've borrowed it from the book Switch by Chip and Dan Heath. It's great, including this parallel I used. Inside the Honda Insight there is a system called Eco Assist. What does it do? First, it has a tachometer. If you take a look inside the car, the one thing that stands out is the central dashboard element—a tachometer with a glowing background. The background color changes with your driving style. When you are driving economically, the tachometer glows green in the Honda Insight.

When you press on the gas pedal, the background glow goes from yellow to brown and orange and finally stops at red, which then means: Dude, you have a whirl in your tank. More or less, this is how it works. It's one of the first and foremost gamification mechanisms. It's called instant feedback.

A player—I'm using this word for anyone who is engaged in your activity—needs to know instantly if he's doing the right thing or if he's doing something wrong. The instant feedback system is what okays the player or gives him the thumbs down if he does something wrong. But this is just the start. Once your driving style follows eco principles, another Eco Assist element activates. In the dashboard display of the Honda there is a small plant called the driving guide. If you're driving economically over a long period of time, the plant gets new leaves. It's a variation on a points system. As you're earning the leaves, earning the points, you are engaged in a game. When I tell people about this system, they go, "Darn, I need just the thing." To be honest, the system doesn't actually make any real sense because you get nothing in return for the leaves, but it does work. It works so well that the solution has also been used in other cars from Ford or Nissan.

If you get inside the new Nissan Leaf, an electric vehicle, you'll see that the plant is now placed centrally on the display on the dashboard. It's a thing to behold. The Honda Insight one I show you is simpler, but the Nissan plant is just beautiful. The leaves are well-rendered, green, and just beautiful. You want to have this plant. You show it off to others. Why does it work? It actually works so well that when I tell people about it, they go, "Right. It could work with me." What conditions us into this reaction?

We are the players

The average teen in a developed country spends about 10.000 hours at school, starting with the elementary school through the end of the middle school. The same teen spends roughly 10.000 hours over the same timespan on all kinds of playing forms and games. This doesn't include just video games. Everything's included, also board games like Ludo, dodgeball and so on. You can tell between a teenager who's at school and a teen who's playing at a first glance. This difference lies in different levels of engagement. People get incredibly engaged in playing. Games engage us on an intellectual level, the rider level. But they also engage us on an emotional level—the elephant level.

'I like it' and 'I'd like that' is a perfect match, a paragon of ideal consumer engagement. Why is it so important? Marketing today sees a crisis in engagement. A consumer is no longer willing to actively participate in your brand. To be honest, he just doesn't care about you. There are very few brands that can enjoy customers who congregate in fan clubs, who are active. A study that was conducted in the middle of 2012 shows that a brand can expect active participation only from about six percent of their target audience on Facebook. Just six percent will click the Like button. Only six percent of your target group will leave a comment. For 94 percent of Facebook users, a very large majority, you are either out of sight or they just don't care. Why is that?

One of the reasons is that the customer today, especially one behind a computer screen, faces a host of digital noisemakers. A digital noisemaker is anything that diverts the attention of the customer from interacting with your brand. For someone who is browsing Facebook, your post is one of the tens if not hundreds of other posts published by brands, family and friends. What do you think? Are you bigger than that guy's friend list? Not a chance. Or at least, not if you're publishing a standard post.

If you don't bring on the fun for your customer, you are not winning his attention. Gamification in essence is a countermeasure that fights this engagement crisis. Digital noisemaking can also mean that even if I wander off onto your fan page, if someone pokes me or drops me a line, a text message or an email, I will close your app and take my toys somewhere else. It's a fight for one screen. Facebook needs to win your screen in a battle against emails, chats, Skype. If you don't engage your customer, you lose him.

The customer will be off to find greener pastures, pastures that give him greater enjoyment from shopping and social interaction. When I started to work in gamification, it used to be explained by what I now refer to as the mechanical definition. Gamification is applying game mechanisms to affect people's behavior in the real world. That's exactly what it was for the Honda Insight. Game patterns were used to change the behavior of people outside the game environment, in the real world.

People started saving fuel naturally, in passing. Imagine what could happen if they started to drop by your coffeehouse or shop by the way. Gamification is a trend that is at the interception of three domains. First, loyalty programs, which we'll talk about more later. Second, consumer behavior psychology. Third, game design. Game design is a field colored by consumer behavior psychology. Marketing on the other hand began to take notice of gamification only when it could be used for loyalty programs. This early mechanical definition is not exhaustive and doesn't cover the basic thing I've learnt about gamification since.

Gamification 1st rule: fun

What's most important in gamification is fun. The definition I now fully agree with is this one: Gamification is ingesting fun into activities and events that are normally not entertaining.

Fun. Keep fun at the top of your priority list when creating gamification. The very last point you have to check before you call it a day is: Is it fun? One hassle I always fight with is that when you add the word 'educational' before a noun, people instantly neglect the fun aspect. An educational game—what's that, really? It's a game that is designed to teach you something. When I consult this kind of projects, I ask people, "Would you play it if you didn't have to?" They go, "No, but it's an educational game." If you wouldn't play it, it's not a game to begin with.

Lectures and talks are much like that. If learning something means tormenting yourself to gain some knowledge, if it's dull and the opposite of fun, that's weak. A good lecture is a lecture that entertains its audience. Same goes for shopping. We no longer compete now in terms of products. This change can be traced back to how the current consumer has evolved. We have been living in prosperity for very long now. The current consumer, in his twenties or thirties, can't recall the time when some products or services had limited availability. When he wants to buy stuff, he's got the entire Internet to rummage for it.

In the sixties marketers identified the four Ps of marketing. This marketing mix explained how brands can shape their competitive practices. To describe this competition, four Ps are used. They stand for Product, Place, Price, and Promotion. The four Ps. Product means competing in terms of products. I have something others don't have. Price is competing in terms of product value. I offer a product at a cut-rate price, or the opposite, at a bigger price. There is a mass of articles that you'd rather buy because they are more expensive. Place: competing in terms of location. I will stop by at your place because your prices are the same, but it's closer. And finally Promotion: what we are used to call marketing. I will buy at your place because for whatever reason you got stuck in my head, your ad got me. If you're running a company, remember to work out a good balance between Product, Place, Price and Promotion.

You need to have a great product. You need to sell it at the right price. It should be easily obtainable with lots of distribution options, and your ad needs to reach your target group. The problem? The market is oversaturated. Imagine this. You crawl out of bed in the morning to buy fresh bagels. A short walk from your place are five different stores or bakeries.

They don't compete in terms of product. They all sell the same kind of bagels that don't differ in taste or size. They don't compete in terms of price. Shelling out a cent or two less isn't worth the fuss of going somewhere else. They don't compete in terms of place. They're all nearby. And they don't compete in terms of promotion. I already know about them. They're all in my head.

Based on what arguments does a well-informed customer in an oversaturated market make a final decision? What do you think? He'll go to a store where purchase is the best experience.

You can work around this idea and say, "That's because the lady who sells bagels has a good rapport with customers," or "It's because the lady at the counter is good-looking." You can say "That's because they recognize me and put away the bagels for me." All this boils down to the fact that I choose this store to buy my bagels. Not because of product, place, price—because of experience. When is this experience at the peak? When it's the most fun. We're back at gamification.

Gamification in real business

In reality, gamification is more than just designing marketing games—although obviously it can be that. Gamification is not a smartphone app—although it can be an app. Gamification boils down to the fun experience. Fun is the secret ingredient that makes it all work. I'll give you an example.

We did a gamification strategy for a pub. How does a pub draw people in? Through product (beer), location, promotion and so on. But it can also look to fun for help. We were to hold a promotion. The standard type. Buy a beer, get one for free. In this promotion, the pub hands out half of its beers for free. How can you bite into this to gamify it? Forget apps and codes. What did we do?

We gave waiters a coin, and then told them: Don't offer customers a free beer if they buy one. It's dull. It's weak. If someone's buying a beer, go to them and invite them to a little game. Let's toss a coin. If you call heads, and it's heads, you win a beer. If it's tails, you pay the full price, as if there was no promotion. People fell in love with this. Now, the costs of this promotion are about the same as the costs of the 'buy one, get one for free' promotion. The toss coin average is fifty percent. You can't bypass the law of large numbers. But what did we see in the pub after three days? It began to sell more beer. Why? It's because if you lose, the first thing you want to do is to even the score. You'll play on until you win. That's a first.

The second thing is a product that advertises itself. In marketing or brand building, there is a concept of a product that can advertise itself. Obviously you can still advertise it yourself, but it shines most when others see it being used. Many brands use this solution to great results. Think of the Polaroid cameras from a long time ago. Your first impression was that this guy is using an apple box to take pictures, and then a picture comes out of it, people crowd around the guy in a park and ask him, "What are you doing?" "I'm using a camera, by this and this brand."

In 2000, when Apple tested the iPod, it also faced the same problem. As a lifestyle item, the iPod should essentially advertise itself. But the worry was that using an iPod means keeping it in a pocket. How did they go round this problem? Steve Jobs approached earbud manufacturers for a white model of earphones. At that time, people thought this was just nonsense. No-one makes white earbuds. But thanks to this, iPod users were able to recognize themselves even if the device itself was hidden in a pocket. White earbuds became a symbol.

The same story was with the beer. When others saw that someone was gambling for a free beer, they said, "Hey, I want in, too! I didn't want to buy a beer but it looks like fun. I want in, can I?" Bottom line, we were selling more beer than ever, and we did this without technology and apps. We simply had a fun idea.

What you have to know about the gamification?

10.000 hours...

Ten thousand hours is more or less the amount of time you spend at school. And more or less this is the amount of time you spend on playing. It appears there's a whole new parallel system different from traditional education that teaches you stuff. Ten thousand is a funny number as well. Malcolm Gladwell, a journalist, the author of popular science books like Blink, dissects the lives of people who have made a difference in his book Outliers. And he does notice something they had in common.

Gladwell believes that ten thousand hours' worth of hard work in a field turns an amateur into a maestro. This would mean that if I, a non-golfer, began to grind my way through the sport, after ten thousand hours of rigorous practice I would be able to dip my toes into prestigious golf tours. I wouldn't win—because at the top, the differences between professionals are a matter of fraction of a percent. It's often about a bit of luck. Still, I would be on a par with the best golfers. If you dedicate ten thousand hours on drudging your way through something rigorously, this will make you a prodigy in the field. So now that we know this, let's think—if ten thousand hours of your life is playing, what do games make you learn? Gaming gives you a certain grounding in trouble-solving. They teach patterns of behavior and approaches that are now being investigated in social sciences.

This is Jane McGonigal, who researches gamers' psychology and motivation. After years of study she was able to come up with several points about gamers' behavior and discovered some differences between gamers and non-gamers. You're probably now thinking I'll talk now about running around with a gun, collecting points and all this. That's inaccurate, because gamer motivation is a lot deeper and more complex. McGonigal's findings are as follows.

The first trait that sets a gamer apart from a non-gamer is a sense of urgent optimism. Urgent optimism is the firm belief that any challenge can be tackled with success. Gamers know that if they try long enough, eventually they will succeed at something that had earlier seemed out of reach. Their experience is living in an environment that has been created uniquely for them. Even if an end goal seems impossible at first—they have to slay a dragon or take on a great sorcerer, gamers realize that if they keep trying, they will be able to it. Nothing is impossible. I'll show you later how this enthusiasm is expressed in the real world.

The second of McGonigal's discoveries is the so-called blissful productivity. It turns out that people can derive satisfaction from the play itself, even if this concept is nonsensical from the point of view of evolution. People waste their valuable resources, energy, we're off guard, we're chasing a stupid ball on a field. All for the sake of fun. It seems that 'fun' doesn't largely fit into the big picture of evolution. But players still want to have fun playing, and will rather go for a little game than sit on a couch and do nothing. They want to put in an effort, and they want it to be fun. If you're skeptical if anyone will take up your challenge if you dare them to make a video or take a stroll someplace, relax. If it is entertaining or exciting, they will do this rather than sit at home and watch television. An entire generation of people now choose to get rid of or never buy a television—unproductive leisure just doesn't do it for them.

The third gamer fact McGonigal found is building up social relationships. Gaming has always been a social activity. Ancient Egyptian monuments have been discovered to bear drawings of primitive games like tic-tac-toe. This implies that when temple guardians grew bored, they would help themselves to a game.

Games have always been a group activity. The playing period that you associate with a lone gamer in a basement or gridlocked room, chopping his way through Diablo all night long, is just a blink of an eye in the thousands of years of gaming. This image is true just for a segment of computer gaming history, and has become dated long ago. Today, a gamer is a social creature. Research shows that you tend to put more trust in people you game with, even they 'kick your ass' so to speak—because gaming requires and implies a fundamental bond of trust.

What is this trust? Many games require players to be in a specific place at a specific time. I have to be sure that you will turn up. I need to trust you will follow rules. If we have played together before, this experience triggers a mind-set of shared trust. This is why games have always been a popular means used to integrate teams and people—if you play with someone, this simply means you trust them. Implicitly, gamers trust each other. This trumps every other benefit: gamers, people who grew up gaming, have much stronger faith in others. This makes a difference for economy and business both.

Gamers are our hope. They have unchecked levels of trust and reliance in each other. A certain completely unscientific study showed that there are two kinds of people who can pick up online a free sleepover or a bed in any city. The first group are owners of Harley Davidson motorcycles. The Harley Davidson bikers stick together so close that if I needed a couch in Barcelona, and was a Harley Davidson biker, I could bank on finding a guy there through my net of contacts who will put me up for a night worry-free.

The other group who can count on getting a free bed in Barcelona are World of Warcraft players. This community is also so tightknit that your network will certainly get you a sleepover anywhere. Think for a moment what kind of credit you would need to be offered free accommodation at a complete stranger's in a city you don't know. Gaming is a great motivator.

An epic win

The last thing I wanted to tell you about speaking of McGonigal's game research is a gamer's sense of an epic win. An epic win is an outcome that appears impossible but you still believe is within your reach. Remember how I told you before about fighting a great sorcerer or slaying a dragon at the end of a gameplay? Gamers believe that their epic win is meant to happen. A well-designed, almost custom-made narrative tops money, grades or any other achievement for gamers.

A belief in an epic win motivates people better than the lure of winning an iPad. Here's an example: Wikipedia. Wikipedia perfectly illustrates all the gamer facts McGonigal came up with. It is a project developed by the gaming generation. An epic win. Let's build an encyclopedia that encompasses all of human knowledge. Let's crush Britannica, Microsoft Encarta and all the other big players in encyclopedias. Is that not an epic win? Sure it is.

But you can't do this on your own. This is a project that has to be opened for a collective effort. Again, it's gamers, people who trust each other, let others edit their articles. They know that anything is possible: just let everyone do their share and get the thing done. This is a perfect example of McGonigal's urgent optimism. The end product is Wikipedia.

You want a proof gamers are behind it? A wiki is a website that invites people to write knowledge articles to it in a certain way. The Wikipedia you know is the world's largest emanation, the biggest instance of a wiki. It contains knowledge articles in over a hundred languages. It's available everywhere around the globe. But do you know what the second largest wiki in the world is? It's the Azeroth encyclopedia. Azeroth is a wiki for World of Warcraft. These guys pay nineteen bucks for playing the game, and share their know-how with others. They write down their knowledge and translate it into 80 languages. It's the second largest wiki in the world: developed for and by gamers.

If you're unsure whether gamers fit into the marketing scheme you are thinking off rolling out with them—believe me, they do. I know that you're thinking I'm just spouting theoretical hogwash. Show me some real examples. Bear with me. I will give you some marketing illustrations later on, but let's now see how this translates into education.

Urgent optimism.

A New York district school launched a fight getting absentee students back to class. The students were teenagers. They don't have to go to school anymore. Well, in theory, they do have to, the law says so, but in practice it's next to impossible to persuade absentees to show up in classrooms regularly. Studies show that simply not skipping classes may have positive effects on a student's results. It's enough to go to school. Students don't even need to work hard to keep at a subject to get some grasp on it. Missing time at school is discouraging and demolishes a student's knowledge.

A small aside: the absolute worst that can happen to a student today is the summer holidays. An eight-week break at the least is eating away at your knowledge. There are tests students take toward the beginning of a school break, and the same tests are taken after the break is over. And what do you know? The results take a distinct plunge.

Back to our New York school, what did it do? The school opted for a scheme where students get points for presence. Not in a digital app. A class schedule was put up on a wall. You had to be present at these classes.

The schedule was filling up as people began to show up. Rewards for effort instead of achievement is something that schools desperately lack. It's effort that should be rewarded. The grades today don't represent effort: they are rewards for accomplishments.

On a similar note, I want to tell you about another key factor, a gamification mechanism. Before, I told you about the instant feedback. Immediate feedback is the part where a gamer is told whether he's going in the right direction, is doing the right thing. Let's now discuss the second element that was used by this New York school. You can use it for your enterprise as well. It's called collections.

What are collections? Imagine you bought chewing gum with a trading card in it. You unwrap the gum, take out the card, you're euphoric by now. "I have a trading card. This is great." Now, what the bubble gum seller should do to 'force' you to buy another package? I call it 'forcing' reluctantly, but what really happens in your head is as good as being forced to buy more gum. He should show you an album with all the cards in a collection.

Now the gears in your head are turning. Your emotional state changes if the collection has in total, say, a hundred cards. You go from "Bless my nose, I have a card" to "I don't have these 99 cards". True, isn't it?

Our brains are conditioned to stockpile and assemble until we have the entire collection. Tell your user that his account is complete in ten percent only, and then guide him, "To complete 15% of your profile, or up to 20%, do this." This scenario is used all the time for social media websites, applications, stickers, loyalty schemes. So this isn't a new concept by any means. Gamification has assembled the concepts that have been circulating for some time in loyalty schemes, game design or cognitive psychology. They are put together under one umbrella term, creating a cohesive set of ideas. Collection plays an important part in it. The students of the New York school were shown a collection. "This month, you can collect forty hours of English." When they came to a class, an hour was filled up. They were looking at a collection, and this made them want to come to school.

The mechanism was the same in the case of the Honda I showed you. It's not like I don't know how many leaves are left to collect. The leaves I win, as you can recall, are filled up on the drawing, while the leaves that I didn't yet get are empty. This is a collection. I need to collect this and this element.

Productivity

Blissful productivity. Indiana University was one of the first universities in America to run a Game Design faculty.

The Game Design courses resemble a semester-long game. There is a set number of points you can earn. Let's say ten thousand. A student needs six or seven thousand points to get credit. Assuming people are naturally lazy and will minimize required effort, this means the lazier lot would go for the six thousand points they need to get credit and then close the door, never to look back at the class. So is this the case? No.

All the students go over and above the minimum. Most of them strive to get the max points, but not all will be able to because the ten thousand points is a threshold set for a reason. It's another gamification mechanism I'd like to talk about. But before, there's something you need to know. The Game Design class is next to the most sought-after at the university. People want to partake because it's fun. But why is the upper limit set to ten thousand points, if you can get credit collecting just six thousand? Mind you, credit is not linked to a grade. You can't get a better or a worse grade. You either pass or you don't. If you collect six thousand, congratulations. All the remaining points are simply there to give gamers a room for autonomy. If I were to pick a definition of a game, it's autonomy in achieving mastery. Out of a number of definitions I will fall back on, this one is really useful to explain this mechanism. Autonomy in achieving mastery. There are manifold tasks you can get points for at Indiana University. Some require a gamer to put in a solo effort. Others will need team work. Some appear suitable for people who thrive working on their own, for instance for people who like to write essays. Others are designed for extraverts, people who are at their best working in a crowd, when they need to give a presentation or be in the limelight. Not all students are equally comfortable in each of the tasks. The autonomy in this system relies on students being free to choose their own path. I struggle with the contemporary school model because it is very linear. If you take some school elements and place them into an enterprise environment, you're doomed to fail.

The illusion of choice

Your customer will demand choice. Even an illusion of choice, but still—choice.

There's no such thing as choice at school. A test asks one question—what year did WWII start? I know where I can find the answer. It's in the book, lying closed on the table. I even know which page I need to open to find it. But I can't look it up: it'd be cheating. There is one correct answer to this question. That's not the case in the real world. It's very rare that only one solution is possible for a given problem. People want choice anyway. If you're planning to deliver good gamification, you need to deliver choice, even if this choice is deceptive. A customer demands choice, but for the most part doesn't really know what he wants.

Case in point. Do you have a favorite eating place? Going to your usual restaurant, do you typically order 'the usual'?

Most people do have their favorite restaurant, and a favorite snack or drink they order. But if you arrived at your table and found a questionnaire saying, "Dear Patron, in order to improve customer service, we would like to know what you would have us do better." You can check all that applies, for example you can put a tick next to 'bigger menu'. Most people check this answer, and then go back to the same place and order the usual. The illusion of choice is a stunt many companies have grown to use expertly. Of course, they can also try to stand out in the market by offering a limited choice of items, but this is gamification we're talking about. Autonomy in achieving mastery.

One great 'illusion of choice' company is Starbucks. Do you know how many different coffee cups you can buy at Starbucks? 64 thousand.

You can order a coffee in this many combinations, by mixing up ingredients, menu items, sizes and so on. Starbucks naturally boasts about its selection. Starbucks employees, at least in the US, before they are recruited as baristas, need to graduate from a Starbucks University. It's called a university, so it sure takes a lot of training. And the 64 thousand, a nearly infinite assortment of coffees, is a number they use to underline their unique market position. But have you been to Starbucks? If you have, you must have seen the menu hanging over the counter. How many items are listed there? Ten? A very large majority pick their drink not from the 64 thousand possible combinations, but from the ten that are recommended at the moment and are in the menu. As far as illusions of choice go, this one is pretty slick.

Keep in mind that gamification cannot mean assigning your users just one path to a goal. I know that if you want to use gamification in a coffeehouse, your goal is to sell coffee. Still, there are very many customers who don't need to drink coffee daily. You can reward them with points for bringing their friends to hang out instead for simply buying lattes. Although you are selling more coffee, those people tend to behave differently than your standard patrons. I'm going to discuss various gamer types later on.

Build a bond

Another pattern is building up social relationships. I sometimes help teachers deploy gamification, or work on gamification with companies. It's a concept that catches on like fire. What this means is that people who need to engage their customers better often realize that gamification is what they were looking for all along. This engagement crisis is cramping especially schools.

What incentives are now offered to an A+ student to make him study for a test with a weaker student? None. Schools focus on individual effort. There's no reward if both of us get good results. There's a reward if I get a good result. It could be worthwhile to introduce the points system used in Indiana. You can get 1000 points on a test for instance. The normal distribution of results will be as usual: part of the class gets great results, most of the class is average, and the smallest percentage is pretty weak.

But what if you told the class that if 80 percent of students receive over 750 points, all the points will be doubled, what would the A+ student do now? The student who cares about his grades the most will approach the weaker student and say, "Hey dude, we need to study together for this test because our results depend on how we make it together." We conducted this experiment at a secondary school. When people realized that they really get doubled points (which they didn't believe in at first), they began to level up and became the best class that year. They weren't aces before—but incorporating a social mechanism into a game means that people really begin to strive for and achieve an epic win.

The last thing you should know about gamification, not only in the context of education but mostly for marketing, is that customers really enjoy doing stuff together. This is true even if you're skeptical. Of course, if you run a coffeehouse, it's natural that people go for a cup together—but they also want to go to a spa or go shopping not only to purchase some products but also to celebrate their social ties. This cerebral habit is called feasting. It's celebrating your social relationships. You should know about this.

If you can engage your customers into doing something together, you'll get an improved bottom line, and the fun you can get from it will also shoot up.

Another thing. An epic win. Again I'll use an education example. It's one of my favorites, and a proof of how important narratives are. I'm going to talk about narrative itself at the end of the course. What does a first-grader want? How do you encourage him to work hard? A first-grader's biggest hero is a third-grader. A dude who knows all the ropes. The first-grader looks up to him in awe. I read that one teacher used to motivate her first-graders to work hard by promising them they'll turn into third-graders by the end of the year if they keep at it. She held out a promise of an epic win, and you know what? The students really tried hard. In end of second semester competence tests, they went neck and neck with an average third-grader.

They weren't technically moved up to the third grade, but the teacher gave them something important: a sense of fun. At the end of the school year, she threw a party for them and named them honorary third-graders. These guys were given a strong sense of achievement.

Does it change anything for your marketing schemes? Don't skip on the narrative. A narrative drives epic wins. Many enterprises I know and work with use gamification on a purely mechanical level, wanting it to give a spur to their loyalty programs. "Let's give people points, make them earn points."

Now, take out your wallet and count all the loyalty program cards you have. You are collecting points just for the sake of collecting points. This isn't fun. The best loyalty programs engage you and entertain you at an intellectual level. Is there a loyalty program you can swear you're having fun with? I don't think there is, or at least there are very few of them. You are only collecting points to get an award. You forget about it. Your engagement is low. I keep on forgetting about my loyalty cards. I don't remember to take them with me because I drive to a gas station to fill the tank and not to have fun with a loyalty program. Good gamification would engage me more. I would focus on the loyalty program itself, and only then see if it's for a cinema or a gas station chain.

So this is it for the basics of gamification. In the next part I will tell you how to get around and deploy it, and give you the nuts and bolts of gamification mechanisms.

Gamification that works – great concepts

The Bottle Bank

To kick off, I want to show you a couple of concepts that prove gamification is alive and kicking, and that it is not complex at all. Gamification does not require programming or software. It's simply about having the right approach to solving a particular problem you and your company are facing. Let's start with non-profits, for instance with Bottle Bank Arcade.

[Watch Bottle Bank Arcade on YouTube]

http://youtu.be/zSiHjMU-MUo

What makes Bottle Bank Arcade tick? First, it's engagement. I don't know if you paid attention to the statistics. A nearby recycling bottle bank was used maybe twice a day, while this bank, the bank that gives people a sense of fun, was used more than a hundred times more often. Go back to the last scenes: middle of the night, students come here after a party to have fun making the right thing: recycling their bottles.

Another thing you should notice is the sound that goes off as a bottle is thrown in. Do you hear it, the 'ummph'? It's the instant feedback. I discussed this concept before. You're doing a good thing, keep at it. It gives you a boost, it's like an epic win. An epic achievement doesn't have to be awe-inspiring. But if you throw in a bottle and the light flashes on, it's exactly what an epic win is.

The Piano Stairs

The other movie I wanted to share is Piano Stairs. The problem these people had to solve was getting fitter. There are standard stairs at the right side, and an escalator to the left. Is it possible to persuade people to use their legs for the sake of their health? How do you do it?

[Watch the Piano Stairs on YouTube]

http://youtu.be/2lXh2n0aPyw

Note that this solution is based solely on the fun people get from the instant feedback. Doesn't it make you think? The stairs wouldn't have the appeal if they didn't advertise themselves the way they do, if they weren't painted like a keyboard or a piano. But what I'm getting from it is the instant feedback. When you stomp on a stair, it starts playing. Did you see how people moved up and down on the stairs for the sake of being in this game? They were jumping over the stairs. So we're coaxing the right behavior out of these people, and they're doing it gladly for fun. This is urgent optimism, unadulterated. For fun, these guys are willing to bust a gut at the stairs rather than go for the escalator.

The Speed Camera Lottery

The last non-profit project I'd like you to see is called the Speed Camera Lottery. It's one of my favorite projects because there's no reason why it shouldn't be introduced in all countries. The legal system gets it wrong with traffic regulations. Drivers are penalized rather than awarded.

Our brains crave rewards. That's the way they work. If no reward is offered, we make it up on our own. If the only thing you can win while driving is a citation, you are likely to think up a prize yourself: I dodged a police patrol or a speed trap. I am speeding, true, but I am great at avoiding the police. But what if we rewarded drivers for keeping within a speed limit?

[Watch the Speed Camera Lottery]

http://youtu.be/iynzHWwJXaA

Focus on the way the instant feedback shows up on the speed sign. It's crucial, but why? The radar determines your speed, but the sign also shows a hand gesture: thumbs up is great, thumbs down is your driving sucks. The rewards we get don't only work on us. We tend to compare ourselves with other players. That's why you can make a great instant feedback system, but you can also fail at it badly. The stuff done around the Speed Camera Lottery is not accidental, it stems from knowledge found in the instant feedback system field.

Instant feedback

A couple years ago, a US power plant decided to try and run a little experiment in a certain smallish town. It gave its customers electric bills with information on power consumption attached. It indicated if you are using up more electricity than your neighbors or if you're using up less. So what's the problem here? Feedback was served in a style that did not fit its purpose. What would you say if you got your electric bill stating in bold, "Congratulations! Your electricity consumption is lower than in all the nearby households."

This means, or at least most of the people who got this feedback thought it means, "I'm cheap, I use less electricity, can't see why I wouldn't keep this bulb on overnight, keep the heater on." The households that were told they were using less power than their neighbors actually amped up their consumption because people started measuring themselves up against others.

The feedback they got was: compared to your neighbors, your result is this high or low. Meanwhile at households that used more electricity than their neighbors, the consumption would not drop at all. These guys were thinking, "Right. My next-doors are wacko environmentalists. I am not them, I won't do the same." The power plant then dumped the previous test group feedback in favor of a new one that included a happy or a sad face in a bill next to a household's consumption level. You're doing something right, or you're doing something wrong. Because of this, the people who got positive feedback would keep at it. The social norm was maintained. At the same time, the people who got a sad face reacted with reducing their energy usage as they judged themselves against an existing social norm and said, "Alright. I fall short. This is bad."

The same mechanism is used for the Speed Camera Lottery. It doesn't come with a feedback that says you're driving faster or slower than anyone else. It has information on your speed. It can be excellent, or it can be foul. Drivers are not weighed up against others, but against a social norm that we want to sculpt. So when you're creating your own feedback, keep this in mind. Comparing gamers doesn't always parlay into great results. We'll talk about this later, when I'll show you another gamification mechanism, a leaderboard.

Commercial applications

Now, what are the commercial applications? We talked about several different mechanisms. One of the core concepts in gamification is a narrative. Go and see the Ribbon Hero 2 website. It's a game Microsoft developed some time ago to make learning Microsoft Office fun. You can install it for free as an add-on for Office 2007 or above. Office 2007 came with a new interface called Ribbon. It has been really well researched but people still complained that a switchover to Ribbon is a pain. So Microsoft came up with a game. In the game, you can pick up Microsoft Office skills as you are playing, completing some tasks and challenges. Challenges are an element of gamification that we are going to broach.

The problem was that the game was not very engaging. People would install it out of curiosity, complete a couple tasks, and then dump it.

What did Microsoft do in the second version? It added a plot. The game wasn't engaging before because people couldn't see a narrative in it, a goal of the game. That's similar to the loyalty program cards you keep in your wallet. You're earning points for no other reason than to have them. This is compelling for our brains for a while as it's has a novelty factor, but it fades out quick.

If you're designing your own gamification, take a page out of Microsoft's book. I don't mean offer people only points first and then add a narrative. No. They learned it the hard way. You don't have to. Create an engaging gameplay. Make it compelling like in Ribbon Hero 2. Ribbon Hero 2 introduces a character, Clippy. Don't know if you remember him—Clippy was featured in earlier Office versions. Clippy has a task. It's epic, obviously. He has to save the word. And he needs your help in this. You can help Clippy as you're completing individual tasks in Office. You're building up your skills by the way, and Clippy goes ahead in the adventure.

Let's now look into the mechanisms of gamification in detail. How do you get on with creating gamification mechanisms? Let's start with the definition of a game. If you want to design a game, you need to know what it is about. Johan Huizinga, the guy who wrote Homo Ludens, defines plays thus. I broke up this definition into individual rubrics. We are going to examine them one by one.

First off, a play is a voluntary activity. If you are forced to do it, it's not a play. On the other hand, every activity can be a play if you do it freely. It's great news. It means that you can turn nearly anything into a play.

Attracting players, or how to encourage people to participate in a game: rules and a gameplay. If the rules of a game are interesting, if you can see people playing outside, people will be attracted to the game. If a game's plot is well-done, people will be attracted as well. You can draw people into a game using a promise of profit, both internal and external. We'll talk about rewards later. What is the crucial element here though? Remember, people don't engage in a game for rewards. Actually, there are people who will enter a game to get an external reward. Win an iPad, win a camera. The problem is these people don't build brand loyalty. They are loyal to a prize they can win.

There's a ton of websites on the Internet for competition nuts. They are co-sharing info: enter here to win an iPad, go there to win an iPod, grab a photo camera here, get a dishwasher there. They enter advertised competitions.

In terms of sheer numbers, you can count them as participants, but in reality very often these guys have no idea what contest they went in for or what brand that was. No loyalty is build. Prizes and rewards are useful to build up a brand range quickly but if the game you're working on doesn't have the appeal to bring people in, prize or no prize, these folks will come, grab the prizes and ride off into the sunset.

Designing gamification

Ask yourself while designing a game: would you play it on your own? Would you play even if no prizes are promised? Is the entertainment factor high enough to attract a user? If yes, go ahead, carry on with the design. But if the answer is no, consider adding to the game or re-designing some elements. According to the definition, a game is a voluntary activity that is separated from the common world with a boundary. This separation is what we refer to in game design as the magic circle.

The magic circle can be a physical location or a state of mine of a player. The magic circle is a playing field for instance. What this means is if there's a line ahead of me, and I cross it over into a playing field, I am entering the magic circle. The magic circle is where the rules of a game apply. When you walk into a field to play soccer, nothing is different in terms of the physical world—but when you're there, you can't touch the ball with your hand.

When you're walking into a golf course, new rules apply in it as well. When you mentally enter a state of playing, for example playing chess with your friend, the world as such doesn't exist there anymore.

There's a place where we both are but above all, a game is a state of mind. I know there are some rules, some behavior patterns I need to follow. My move, his move. Some pieces can be moved, others can't.

One of the ways that separate the common from the unusual, that separate the worlds, is a gameplay. First, there is a location: you can persuade a player to physically walk into a specific place. The place is the world of the game then. When a guy walks into your bar, your store, they accept the rules of your game. That's physical. On the other hand, a player can be in a mood for a game but not physically in the place you want him to be. So you can create a mental game, using a narrative. You can tell the player, "Your situation is this, and these rules now apply."

Also, you can use totems. A totem is anything that advertises your game in the real world. Totems are a big thing. See, why Apple computers come with apple stickers? The company thinks you are likely to put the sticker on your bumper, on your desk, or on a notebook. It's another of the products I told you about—a product that advertises itself. More often than not, totems imply that a player has specific rights in a game and some specific duties. Consider queuing. Standing in line is a game per se. People join lines freely. And there are rules to follow as well. I can't cut in line. I can't push my way through it. I need to enter the line at the end. Being able to skip a queue can be something people are willing to pay for.

Think about airline loyalty programs. If you have a Diners Club card, one of the benefits this card has is waiting-free check-in at airports. People are willing to pay for that.

This totem—the card is a prime example of a totem—when is it reaching its full potential? It's at the peak when besides faster service, you are getting better status. People often enter a game to win status. What is it? Status is about being able to march right next to a queue, boasting, "Look, I am better than you lot." I could be checked-in without waiting at a different desk, at the other side of the airport, but this wouldn't be as fun. Airlines know this. They roll out a red carpet, or an equivalent of a red carpet, next to a normal gridlock of people. Banks do the same thing. It's a game, really. My credit card gives me early access to concert tickets. For example American Express provides its customers with exclusive access to tickets.

If you want to engage people in a game, give them status or access. They are internal game rewards. Access, for instance, is extremely desired as rewards go, and doesn't cost you a thing. A certain fashion house holds regular midnight sales. It gets rid of clearance items at reduced prices. Shoppers will queue for the sale, much like are willing to stand in line for the opening of a new J&R. So what does this fashion house do to reward their loyal customers? It gives them access to a closed store fifteen minutes before the rest of the queue. Shopaholics are willing to pay through the nose for this, for instance lay out a thousand dollars a month to get access to these midnight sales. I'm making up this number just in case you're asking. Anyway, fashion houses really offer this perk to loyal shoppers. You can go in fifteen minutes before everyone else, get the best deals, and only after you're done the rest of the crowd storm in. You know what's the best about this? All these chicks with their noses pressed against windows while you're picking the best of the clothes fifteen minutes earlier. Isn't this fun? People will want to pay for that.

There are a lot of instances of totems and games that are separated from the common world. A courtroom, for example, is definitely a game. I enter the magic circle. Inside it, there's a guy in a funny wig. He is the power itself. He doesn't have power over me in any other sense, but when I'm entering enter the courtroom, I enter the magic circle, and I have to obey his authority. I have to stand up when I'm addressing him. Silly, isn't it? I have to be quiet, because he tells me to. I have to call him His Honor and so on.

Corporations are exactly the same. Employees have to follow a dress code, don a uniform. Some totems are power symbols: I can walk next to all the cubicles in an office holding a golf club. This is my power symbol. Not everyone in the office can do it. If you can design a game that rewards people by giving them more benefits and privileges over different groups of customers, it will not cost you a lot. Your customers on the other hand will be willing to pay a small fortune to boost their status.

Another element in the definition of a game is rules. Rules that you accept freely: if you enter a game, you agree to obey a set of rules. It's worth here to take a look into a certain type of gamers: the non-gaming gamers. These people are reluctant to follow rules. There are kinds of people who don't want to follow rules. The first behavior you need to pay attention to is exposing the magic circle. It happens when a guy walks into a playing field, grabs the football and says, "Hey, it's just a game." Gamers hate them. They want to play, and if someone exposes the magic circle for some egotistic reason (because for example he's bad at kicking the ball), you only need to wait for the rest of the players to get rid of him. They will do it themselves, more or less democratically. They will ostracize him. It only spells trouble if the guy is able to continue spoiling the fun because there is no-one to kick him out of your virtual field, push him out of the virtual queue if he cuts in line. This means you need to provide for a gatekeeper of sorts inside your game. Not one gatekeeper, but an institution that protects the rules and acts like a referee on a sports field, deciding whether or not you can stay in a queue.

It decides whether or not you can be invited to a store before everyone else, or if you can buy this product at a reduced price or not. This is what this is about.

The other type of a gamer is someone who tries to defeat the system using the rules. It's called gaming the game or gaming the system. Let's go back to the fashion house. Some time ago I was standing in line in a store in this chain. They had a special promotion on. For every ten dollars spent, you'll get a small gift. A lady standing ahead of me in line wanted to purchase items for nearly thirty dollars. She read up about the special offer at the counter and added some cheap item to the basket to make the purchase total over thirty. She seemed to imagine that if every ten dollars means a gift, then thirty dollars will give her three freebies. Seems alright. It doesn't go against the rules of the game. When her turn came, she put the items on the counter and said, "These cost over thirty dollars. Three pairs of socks, please." The check-out assistant went, "No, the promotion is for a single receipt purchase, if you spend over ten dollars at a time, you get just one prize." So what did the lady do? Think about what you would do. She asked for three receipts. You can't say it's against the rules. She was keeping the rules. She didn't cheat. She only wanted to make the most of the offer. To exclude this player, a player that is taking full advantage of a rule but doesn't flout it, is the absolute worst you can do.

Tesco was in a similar position some time ago. They came up with a game (they think of something each year as far as I remember). A customer who has the longest till receipt wins a prize for his school as Tesco has had a local school support program. What did people do? They were buying small items for peanuts, and then asked check-out assistants to scan the products one by one. And so the receipts were of course twenty feet long. This isn't cheating as such. Yes, Tesco doesn't like it as it makes queues longer and cashiers dog-tired, and doesn't bring a profit for them. The receipts are huge, but the idea for the game was different. At any rate, punishing a gamer for creativity is the worst that can happen. If Tesco excludes a gamer from a play because he thought up a great way to get a long receipt without paying more, it's an own goal. This applies to you as well. Remember: a game is autonomy in achieving mastery.

These guys stepped up their creativity. They went for less trodden path but stuck to the rules you gave them. Penalizing them for this is a bad, bad idea. What can you do instead? Make them co-operate with you. Obviously, you are free to change the rules in-game if you see they are abused but you can't punish people who clued you in to this. It is your flawed rules, not their creativity that brought this. Keep this in mind.

Another factor is motivation. Entering a game can be motivated with a promise of an internal reward—the fun of gaming itself—or with external rewards. As for internal rewards, the rewards of a game, there's a model called SAPS. It was developed by Gabe Zichermann, one of the cool guys in gamification. SAPS stands for Status, Access, Power and Stuff.

Status is something we discussed before. People are willing to game to be better than others. It's like the military. The military is a great illustration to the claim that a status of a person is apparent on the outside. At barracks, it takes a glance to know who's above me and who's below. The telling signs are of course epaulettes. People are willing to fork out a tidy sum for status alone. You don't buy a Ferrari to drive your briefcase to work. Ferrari is a status symbol. You spend a small fortune on a car that is strictly speaking non-drivable. You won't be able to through New York, Washington or Los Angeles in a Ferrari to get to your workplace or break the speed limit in any way. You will be held up in traffic jams all the time—but once you pull in at work, you're the only one with a Ferrari. Just you. This is the reward you're paying for in the first place.

Next, Access. I told you about access before as well. People will pay to get early access to stuff. If you want to boost the appeal of your game, the one thing you can try is to allow a group of customers to access stuff they like in advance, before others. It's about closed tests, beta applications, entering midnight sales before others or access to private facilities such as a VIP airport lounge. Apart from prompt service, a Diners Club card gives you access to VIP lounges at airports. Where's the entrance to a VIP lounge by the way? Next to the standard departure hall. Sure, I could use a back entrance, but if I did, who would notice? So I'm going past all the riffraff. You can watch me but you can't come with me. You don't have the access. This is what Access is all about.

The third thing people are willing to pay for—or at least focus on in a game you create for them—is Power. If you give people Power, they will stick to it.

Perhaps you'd been so active on a message board that you were eventually given a mod status. It doesn't cost anything to create mods. What's more, you are cleaning up on the behalf of an administrator. He'd have to do all the work himself anyway—but the knowledge that they were selected out of many to help with the board, that they have power over other users, makes mods and administrators the most loyal of customers.

Imagine what would happen if you let a customer manage a queue. Let people skip the line or make them wait at the end. While you may believe that chaos would ensue, instead it's urgent optimism that emerges. Gamers are willing to play and obey the rules, and they want to do what they're told. If you give them Power, for the most part they will use this power for good. Think about what you can offer your gamers—what previously was reserved for your staff only for example. Power will make people engaged.

Note that the SAPS model places Stuff, the actual standard prizes, at the far end of the definition block. Why is that? Stuff, like I said at the begging, pulls you in but to a lesser extent. You don't want to play to get stuff, you want to play to get the internal rewards of a game. The rewards—Power, Status, Access—are what holds varied levels of interest for various types of gamers.

The next thing you should keep in mind while creating a gamification scheme for your company is that not everyone will play for the same stuff. There are people who get motivated using a different array of solutions. So how do you split gamers up? This will be the next subject.

How to engage customers?

Motivation

What makes gamers play? Not all players who are engaged in your game are playing for the same reason. I'll tell you about someone called Richard Bartle. Back in the eighties, Bartle researched the first communities of gamers. Where did the dug them up from? He had a contract at a university and designed the one of the first, if not the first MMORPG, a type of a game that is just like the ones I told you about, for instance like World of Warcraft.

Bartle's RPG was called Multi-User Dungeon. It was essentially a text-based game. The students who had access to a terminal could use it to visit virtual worlds and interact with each other. Bartle soon took notice that these interactions would differ with different people: not everyone did the same stuff in games and not everyone behaved the same. He began to try to discover the underlying motivations of players and eventually found out that are four basic preferences players can have.

The first motivation is in-game rewards. The second appeal is exploring the game world, the third—socializing with others. The fourth metric is power, exerting power over others. Based on his findings, Bartle developed one of the first and classic player type classifications. This classification borrows from character theory and from psychological types developed by Jung and others, but is revamped to be player-oriented. You have your own player identity as well if you're a player. What types are we talking about? How did Bartle pigeon-hole players?

Types of players: Achievers

The first and the most common player type is Achiever. Achievers single-mindedly strive to be as good as possible in filling the roles and tasks a game gives them. They want to be better than others. These guys love being compared to other players. This is the number one appeal factor for them. This player type is fundamental and the most popular out there, reaching about 70% of gamer population.

Why is that? It's because if I decide to play a game, the first thing I do is to follow the rules set out for me. I am rewarded if I do this. I earn points, badges, achievements. This is fun. At some point further on I'm itching to look for more advanced scenarios, but most games cater to this basic player type, a player that is engaged through the use of points and achievements. We'll look into this later.

Types of players: Explorers

The second player type is Explorer. Explorers thrive when they can 'unlock' a game and see through all its secrets. They live and game for knowledge. If they can level up more quickly, if there's a hidden shortcut, they will want to know about it.

Remember the psychology types aren't just about games. An Explorer is not just a gamer. Explorers can be people who use Photoshop knowing all the keyboard shortcuts ever. It's a person who boasts about knowing the best café around town. It's someone who can give you a tour of the city's top fashion outlets.

Explorers are guys who feel best if they can show off their knowledge, and they excel if you feed them facts and nuggets of information they can rave about. If you're running a coffeehouse and want Explorers in your loyalty program, you can't do much better than give them for instance a coffee encyclopedia. Give them knowledge and let them share knowledge with you. If they approach you with some tidbit about coffee, put in in the encyclopedia. They will be proud that they can be part of this. I'm using encyclopedia as an example only but keep in mind that these gamers are knowledge-driven.

Types of players: Socializers

Next in line we have Socializers. Socializers are players who see a game simply as a means to create and build social relationships. Remember, this is not just about games per se. Socializers are people who hang out at coffeehouses (I'm bouncing back to the coffeehouse example because it fits a business context) not to have a cup but to see their friends. Socializers are guys who play chess or poker not to win but rather to have a chat, ask a friend how things are. How's wife and kids?

For them, the game is an excuse. It's just an occasion to interact with others. They thrive if they can show off their network of friends and relationships. You can design in-game tasks for them as well. If you have a loyalty program, you can for example make it include tasks that target Socializers. The task should be "Book a party at our place for ten people" rather than "Buy lots of lattes," if we're still using a coffeehouse as an example. That is what Achievers can be engaged by. A Socializer doesn't want to buy coffee for the sake of it. He needs social relationships more. If you tell him to get a fixed number of people together at your place, he'll do it.

Types of players: Killers

The last player type Bartle classified is Killer. Killers are a curious bunch because these guys don't game to win. They game so that others will lose. The biggest appeal for them is power—power over other people and other players, the ability to influence others. If you don't channel this aspiration into the right direction, Killers will tie you up. But if you let them use their power harnessed in the right way, they will be the best gatekeepers you can wish for. Killers are guys that can make great mods, great gatekeepers and in-game police of all sorts.

Exerting power over other players and the power to remove them from a game is the number one factor why Killers will be engaged in your activity and will carry on the tasks you give them. The tasks don't have to be major. Take a look at Facebook. It has a little bit of something for everyone. For Killers, the main incentive is Report a violation or Report a user. As a Facebook user, I know I have tangible power over the community. If a user is reported enough times, he will be removed or banned. This can happen to legitimate celebrity profiles as well. Killers gang together and report a page as offensive or illegitimate. When a threshold for these complaints is reached, the page will simply be removed. Talk about power. Power can be malicious and undesired if it is not channeled correctly, but once you put it to a good use, Killers can be a great help.

Mechanics and game dynamics

Let's now go into game mechanics and game dynamics. The two concepts are communicating vessels that make a game work. Dynamics is the plot of a game, while mechanics are the underlying mechanisms that make gameplays work. Dynamics can be for instance rewards, while the mechanisms that make rewards work are points and feedback. Dynamics is for instance status. It's a player who gains on status and position in a game. The mechanism that makes this possible is levels.

A game gives me a boost, a satisfaction of having completed a mission. A mission in game dynamics is an achievement. But it's a challenge that makes you complete a mission. We challenge players to something and they accept it and complete the challenges. Next on, there's competition. Like I said before, some gamers thrive on competition, on comparing themselves against others. A basic competition mechanism is a leaderboard of people who have different scores. You can compare yourself against them. There are also players who don't enjoy competition. They thrive on co-operation. Socializers fit this image best. This co-operation dynamics is possible if you can offer gamers mechanisms such as gifts, tasks like 'do something for others', generosity and so on.

Other similar constructs are voluntariness, mastery, expressing yourself. They are all about dynamics. You can add to this dynamic by using for instance avatars, although game research shows that they should be used with caution if at all.

 In reality, if you designing a ground plan for a game there are just two safe applications of avatars (I'm now adopting some game design research). The first application is children's gamification. Kids relate to an avatar very strongly. They will customize the avatar to reflect themselves. I showed you before what a kid does when he gets an Xbox. The kid customizes his avatar, gives it the right hairdo, body shape, clothes, shoes. An adult couldn't care less to be honest. Adults can just imagine what their avatar looks like, without needing a crutch of a physical representation. They just don't need that.

Another use of an avatar, a player's physical representation, that makes sense are applications related to serious problems a player can't cope with. Problems that aren't internalized. This is how soldiers with PTSD can be rehabilitated. A gamified therapy shows some events and episodes the soldiers experience in the real life—but it's their avatar, a representation, that is in the game instead of them. Avatars are very useful if you need to separate yourself from your emotional side, for example in therapy. But if you're a brand and have a website where you can create avatars, buy a necklace or earrings and so on for an avatar—most people aged over 14 will not go for it. If you're marketing toward adults, people who pay—depending on your target group—avatars are next to useless.

Points. Let's talk about the techniques and methods for using points to full advantage. We already talked about some. What do you need to know about points? First off, points are used best if they are in a collection. Remember what I told you about sticker albums? Having a point doesn't spark your imagination, but ten points is really something. Businesses seem to have realized this for their loyalty programs. I don't know if you have ever used a car wash or had a lunch at a joint that runs a dining loyalty program. When you buy a salad at these places, a nice lady hands you a card and says, "The eighth salad is on us. Here, have a stamp."

Car washes often use the same idea. I have my car washed and get a card: the eighth wash is free. The problem is that with the first coupon, the first stamp for a salad or a wash, my motivation is still low. Psychologists have come up with some tips on fighting this crisis. You need to show your customer that he's close to the goal: not at the start but actually already on his way to it. The beginning of a long road is daunting. So if you want to use this marketing scheme, you shouldn't tell you customer, "Eight stamps are a free wash, here's the first stamp." You should tell him, "Ten stamps are a free wash, you already have three." The customer is less likely to dump the card in a nearby bin if he has three stamps than if he had just one.

The next thing to tackle is naming your collection. You can't do much worse in your game, loyalty program or anything else you're designing for your brand, than to dub points 'points'. That's weak.

Not creative. Take out your wallet. How many cards do you have that encourage you to collect points?

You can earn 'points' in each of the programs. So how do you make your brand, your product, even if it's a loyalty program or a marketing game, stand out if it has the same drab name as everything else? On a similar note, you need to remember to define a good reinforcement scheme.

Reinforcement schemes

What are reinforcement schemes? There was a guy called B.F. Skinner, one of the first people who worked on a reinforcement theory. What did Skinner find out? First off, there are two kinds of reinforcements: continuous and random. Secondly, in order to get rewarded, you can do two things. You can be rewarded for effort and rewarded for outcome, your results.

How do you merge the two rewards to create the best engagement possible? In continuous reinforcement, the reward is tangible. I know what I need to do to get it. I am rewarded for effort, and this has a great appeal. Let's go back to the coffeehouse I keep bringing up. Imagine that it has a special offer: buy five coffees, get the next one for free.

I buy the first cup, the second, and the third. My engagement is pretty high. I tell myself there are only two cups left. If I have a choice between this coffeehouse and a different one, I'll choose my usual place because I know that if I order two coffees more, I'll get the fifth one free. Playing for a coffee is kind of pathetic in terms of rewards, but you might think up something better. But once I have been rewarded with the free coffee, what's left of my motivation then?

The next day, if I need to choose between the two cafés, I have no reason to go back to the old one. I've got my free coffee. To get another one, in both places I'd need to buy five cups again. What can you do to counteract this? One way-out is creating a reward scheme that works like an umbrella. How does that work, exactly? You reward the same effort with multiple prizes over a longer time horizon. What does it mean? It means that while buying five coffees gets you a free cup, three visits more mean getting, I don't know, a bigger cup. So when I am gratified with the fifth coffee and I don't plan to return, actually I'm already half-way in to win a bigger cup. And once I have received that bigger cup after eight calls, I only need two more to get another free drink, and about twenty more to get for instance a glass mug.

The same activity is rewarded with increasingly bigger prizes over a stretched time horizon. Thanks to this, after I have received the first prize, my motivation still has a pulse. I'm likely to come back to the coffeehouse. When you're designing your own loyalty program, your reward scheme needs to be covered under an umbrella platform.

Random rewards can be used as an extra spur. A random reward is actually offered up for nothing. It's unbalanced, unexpected, and doesn't correspond to your effort. Imagine you walk into a coffeehouse and the barista tells you, "You're our thirteenth customer today, on Thursday, so you get a coupon for ten coffees" or something like that. You were not aware of this rule before, but the fact that there are hidden rules you can uncover sparks up your imagination.

You keep going back. What will happen if I go there at two in the morning? What happens if I bring three of my friends around? There should be a multitude of random rewards but preferably distributed over various different places and related to player challenges. A challenge to bring your friends, a challenge to drink a specified amount of coffee drinks, a challenge to add an entry to a coffee encyclopedia. Why? To make all types of players catered to. To make them explore. This is an idea that works well with the second type of players, with Explorers.

Note that if you are rewarding users for effort, higher levels need to be linked with increased effort from a player. It's not quite like you are getting more experienced in the game. If you get a free coffee as a gift for the first visit in a coffeehouse, great. But you can't get a free coffee with the next call. It'd spoil you in no time. With the next visit, you need to be expected to put in more of an effort, and at the third level you should still try harder. If people are willing to play for status and access, the challenges you set for them have to be increasingly harder.

Otherwise, their engagement plummets. Once they notice a challenge is too easy, their engagement will drop. So if you're designing challenges, remember about reward schemes and their core concepts.

The next mechanism is levels. I bit off this topic before as well. Levels indicate a player's status. If through a level you are able to exert an influence over other players, it is a power symbol. Levels hit the highest point when people can see each other's results. Remember military epaulettes? Now, how can you make players statuses visible for them as they are interacting? How can you make your employees tell—even the new staff—right away that a guy who's just walked into a store has to be served without waiting? What can you give that person? What totem can be outwardly evident for everyone and influence other players' behavior?

You can hand out special Café Friend badges. If a guy wears it on his chest your staff knows they need to give him top service, serve him first or give him coffee in a glass mug rather than a paper cup. This doesn't cost a lot but the status of this patron will be obvious for everyone in the coffeehouse. He is like your human billboard. He'll talk about your place with others. If I wear a badge on my jacket to a workplace or anywhere else, people will take notice. "Hey, what's that badge? Where is it from? What does it mean?" And I will very gladly put them in the know. "Look, this badge means I get served first. It means I get a glass mug when every other guy gets coffee in a paper cup."

What does it to take to get one? You need to buy twenty cups at the coffeehouse. While this isn't strictly epic, that's what it takes. A lot of businesses big and small do it. Platinum cards or black cards are a great example of totems. Everyone can get them, provided they fit some rubrics. You need to have a fixed amount of money on your account, sometimes it's a tidy sum. You need to keep the money on the account. But to gain this status and to derive satisfaction from being able to show it off, people are willing to make all sorts of sacrifices. Think for a moment about the products you are buying to make everyone see you can afford them.

Do you have a Ferrari? It doesn't to have be a Ferrari but there's a ton of small gadgets we buy to show off our status. You might persuade yourself that a Chanel flap bag is the best thing ever but it will hold your phone just like a bag for 20 or 50 dollars will. But it is the best thing ever as far as status symbols go. Louboutin shoes with their trademark red soles. A product that advertises itself and is a status symbol at the same time. Very often the price is the repellent, or a barrier, but it doesn't always have to be the case. If you have a cheap product to sell, what you are giving people—the fifty or the hundred coffees—is the leg-up that moves them a level up in a status ladder.

Challenges

Gamification also makes use of challenges. Challenges are what gives a player satisfaction from a game. They impact your reward system in a powerful way. The reward system is in your brain. Satisfaction from having completed a task is driving the internal satisfaction. If you don't keep people updated with new challenges, the satisfaction will start to drop—or they will come up with a challenge on their own. Isn't it what you did as a kid? Walking on sidewalks is boring, so you would challenge yourself. Balance the curbs and don't fall. This stuff goes straight to your brain's pleasure center. It's fun. When you grow up, you don't do this anymore, maybe with some exceptions. But this is great because you challenge yourself and feel gratified if you succeed. In a supermarket, you challenge yourself to pick the fastest-moving line. Satisfaction from a well-done task is something that drives people. If you don't make a room in your marketing scheme for challenges, your customers are likely to come up with them on their own.

Challenges have a clear-cut structure. A definite end-goal. But how do you design them? Stick to your reward scheme. I already reviewed this concept. An umbrella scheme. Have several concurrent challenges you make your players follow in several different time horizons. Ten coffees is a cup, 50 coffees means no waiting, 100 means you get your own mug in the coffeehouse and so on. Have several different dynamics.

Challenge your players to show up at a specific place at a fixed date. Come and grab your coffee before 9 am. Bring two friends on a Thursday. There is an awful lot of things people are going to do if they have a fixed goal ahead of them. The more challenges you set, the longer player satisfaction will last. That's why folks give up on collecting points. The satisfaction they derive from is short-term. I got a card, it's fantastic. I collect and collect and collect. But the end it turns out it's not very fun after all.

Leaderboards

Gamification can also use leaderboards that let you see the results you have and compare them with others' results. It's a great incentive for Achievers. There are some things you should know before you create a leaderboard. First, it's the social aspect.

Remember how I told you about getting into a car that welcomes you with a quip, "Your brother-in-law Mark consumed 2.2 gallons on the same trip you're taking"? It wouldn't make the same impact if the voice said, "Larry Loe from the East Coast, you wouldn't know him anyway, burnt 2.2 gallons on this trip." Social aspects of information is relevant. If you can measure up players against their friends rather than a bunch of folks they don't know, show them a leaderboard they can relate to. This will motivate them to move up.

Remember about baby steps. If my result in a game is 20 points, and the guy at the top of the leaderboard has hoarded 20 million points—sorry, this doesn't motivate me at all. Knowing there's a leaderboard like this out there is not encouraging or motivating in the game.

Now, what could encourage me? The leaderboard should say, "Great, you have twenty points." A guy above you, who could be your brother-in-law or an anonymous face, has twenty-four. It doesn't take a lot to beat that guy. The best games are going to show you a leaderboard that is customized for the social aspect, show you your friends instead of random best players—unless you're the upper crust of the game yourself, in that case you want to know the whole leaderboard. They should display only this fragment of the leaderboard that is relevant for you. What would that be? Obviously, the one you are sandwiched in. You want to see the guy who is below you so that you know you're not the worst, and the guy above you, so that is gives you a spur to continue in the game and have a defined goal—beat the guy above you.

To give you an example of an application that really gets it—Nike+. You can set a challenge online and then invite your friends to it. You can challenge your friends to cover a distance of 50 miles over a week and track who's first. It's a challenge for runners. Having a clear goal is a very strong motivator. Second, you can earn points—miles you run in this variation. Third, there are collections. Miles don't appear out of the blue, there is a collection you are filling. You need to collect 50 miles. Fourth, you can see how your friends are doing in this view. I challenged four friends and can see their progress in real time. I can see who's at the top, where I fit in, who is third and so on. To keep my place, I need to run this many miles today. To catch up with the current winner, I need to run this hard. This is what it looks like and it works like a charm.

I don't know if any of you have used Nike+. It's an application that helps athletes keep their motivation going. It has a fantastic instant feedback system. The leaderboard I showed you is great in its own right, but has another feature that makes it even better: the instant feedback. If the reward for a challenge is, say, a free lunch on Saturday—the last to the goal is buying—imagine what's going through my head when I wake up in the morning and need to put on my running gear.

If I didn't have this app, I'd open my eyes and go—the elephant inside me goes, "Paul, it's cold outside. There is no part of your body that you can move. Don't do this." But I switch on my phone and it says that Joe, who I challenged myself and who is above me, or worse, just behind me in the leaderboard, is now clicking away the miles. He's catching up with me. So what do I do? Limp over for my running shoes. This is the whole idea.

Gifts and generosity.
The next-to-last mechanism I am going to tell you about. Gifts and

generosity. This mechanism is what motivates Socializers. Many people see a game as a means of influencing others. But they don't do this to sow destruction. Rather, they want to have a positive impact on others. They are playing altruistically, helping others as they go.

A good example of this is Facebook's game du jour in 2010 or 2011, FarmVille. FarmVille is catered to appeal to all player types. If you need jogging your memory, the tasks in FarmVille are to manage a farm, harvest your crops at the right window of time and so on. You earn points for this and can purchase stuff for them—that's the very basic gist of the game. Achievers are playing FarmVille to make their farms bigger than the farms of their friends. To have more cattle, more pigs, bigger fields and so on. Achievers compare themselves with their friends.

But what does a Socializer see in FarmVille? Socializers don't care about having a bigger farm than others. You know that if you can't harvest your crops on time, because you're at a meeting at work, you can ask your friends for a favor. This is how friends can be made. A Socializer is going to play FarmVille not to get the best results, but to get enough cash to buy a baby lamb he can't have at his farm (because it's a special type of a baby lamb or a baby tiger or anything else) and to gift it to one of his friends. This is a way of saying: you matter to me. People express their emotions in this way.

If you can coax your customers into buying stuff for others in your marketing program, not for themselves, it means you are ready to engage them using the gifts and generosity mechanics.

The last gamification mechanism I wanted to cue you in are avatars, which were mentioned in brief some time ago. Avatars and the third place. The third place is a concept developed by a guy called Ray Oldenburg, an architect and urban planner who worked in city and urban area planning. Oldenburg concluded that we all spend a bulk of our lives inside three fundamental environments.

Number one space is home. It's a space we want to be in, a heavily personalized space we spend most of our time in, a space that is ours. The second space is the workplace. It doesn't have to be the workplace only, and can include college, school and so on. If I were to define it, I'd call it a place you have to be in, a place you can't make your own to a large extent, you can't shape its ambience and look. It's out of the question to bring flowers or small accessories and fixtures to your college. The third place according to Oldenburg—he didn't even give it a name other than 'the third place'—is what I'd call a home away from home. It's a place you want to spend your time in and want to make it fit your needs, but it is not yours per se.

If you have your own locker in a gym, you can keep your stuff there and plaster it with your photographs. If you allow people to customize this space, they are going to pay you back with fostered engagement. If you create a game where the reward is status, one of your status symbols can be allowing people to have their own little space in an otherwise public area. Allowing players to express themselves is always going to pay back. This is what players want. I told you about glass mugs for a reason. A glass mug can be a way to show off your status, to tell others you're above them. Now, go one level up. A glass mug with your name on it. Yours only. No-one else will even lay a finger on it. It's a status symbol that you crave to have, but will only achieve it quite far along in the game as coffeehouses simply can't afford keeping exclusive mugs no-one drinks from for the most of the time. But knowing there's a piece of you in a common environment, in your 'own' coffeehouse, is what will drive people. They are willing to go to a great length to get that.

If you're developing a gamified loyalty program, a gamified brand awareness campaign, a gamified way for engaging your customers to do stuff they are now reluctant to do, the ability to customize your offer is something people are willing to spend an arm and a leg on. In a nutshell, these are the gamification mechanisms. You need to merge them and combine them to create a great solution that will engage people. I hope I've given you food for thought and an inspiration. In the next part, we are going to take a look at different types of games. I'll tell you about building fun using narratives, because it really makes all the difference in the world. Using a narrative to create fun.

Bringing gamification into action

Play forms

What are the play forms and the play types? You can break down an activity you are engaged in into four basic aspects. We have as follows: first, a play form that is called Agon (all the Greek comes from Huizinga's Homo Ludens). Agon is a play based on competition, with a classic winner and loser dichotomy. A race, the Olympics Games, sport are all classic plays built around competition. The next play form is Alea. This term includes all games of chance, lotteries and so on. The outcome of these games is strongly influenced by a random element of chance. They have their appeal as well. Gamblers stationed in front of a one-armed bandit in a casino are the best proof that this play form can be really addictive.

Next in line are plays that you wouldn't call plays as such. They're called Mimesis, and they are based on mimicry. Players attempt to imitate someone else. The element of Mimesis in games is role-playing. There are entire classes of games that are built around it: Rope-Playing Games that can be played also outside the virtual reality and at urban areas. The last of the lot is Ilinx. The goal of Ilinx as a play is to overcome the self, to change. It doesn't need winners or losers. The thing you battle is your own weakness. It is a highly addictive play form. You just can't win. Show me a person who's won at Tetris. There's no such thing as winning at it. But there is a multitude of people who are willing to spend hours and hours attempting to beat their last best result, to beat themselves. Fighting anyone else is not necessary in this scenario.

One play form can include several play types. Let's look at dancing. In its classic form, dance is Mimesis. Dancers want to imitate masters, copy their moves. But if you put competition into it, the Agon, you have a dance competition. You can battle yourself, dance to achieve a level, pass an exam. I don't know how randomness fits into dancing, but it can be a judge's verdict or a choice of a group. Classic sport tournaments introduce draw procedures. In soccer for instance teams are drawn from pots to determine which group they will be in. Mixing up play types is what can make your players emotionally engage in your game.

Creating a marketing play with mostly or solely Agon, or competition, in mind, where the classic game will be the number one element, is a misunderstanding. This just doesn't work like that. Mixing up more than one activity type will help you increase the engagement of your users.

Critical elements

The two critical elements in a game are narrative and fun. Why? People desire to experience emotions. We no longer compete in terms of Product, Place, Price or Promotion. Our offer has to include Experience. What does experience stem from and who can deliver a great experience? People live through experiences. That's why we crave it on a visceral level: we want to live through something. Live it emotionally, release our feelings. The outcome of this is that we engage in some brands and products because we feel they give us a better experience. This experience can be a by-product of interacting with other customers or of communication as such. The Cluetrain Manifesto came out in 1999. The authors of this manifesto anticipated the rise of Internet-based communities. They predicted the emergence of social media, and knew that in the future we would communicate more intensely than ever before. The book claims that markets are a different beast that one you have been told about in traditional economy models. If you studied management, economy or marketing at a brick-and-mortar college or university, you were told that markets are the transactions that occur in it. That's not strictly true. A marketplace has never been just about transactions.

We've been swayed to apply the term 'market' to a virtual entity, but it has transformed from a real, specific place. The background is a market square. Why did people gather around in market squares? Was it just for trading?

No, and likewise, modern customers don't go to shopping malls just do buy stuff. Most people go there to window-shop, to gossip, and to exchange views and experience. It was like that at market squares.

Before you bought a coconut, you wanted to have a chat with the coconut seller. People came to share knowledge and experience with others. Selling and buying was a by-product. This is what The Cluetrain Manifesto authors hint at; in a post-industrial, post-transaction age we are going back to that earlier model of trading.

Very often people are hungry for stories. Markets are conversations, The Cluetrain Manifesto claims. If markets are conversations, the brands you create, the brands for which you create gamification, are stories on the markets. What you go for in creating gamification is building up engagement. Let's go back to the beginning. We are experiencing a general drop in the ability to be engaged. People don't engage emotionally in brands because they're stymied with a raft of digital noise makers. So how you can help them become absorbed with your marketing game or a loyalty program? The side-effect of engagement will be increased sale. But first, you need to create a story. If brands are stories, this begs the question: What will be told and how will it be told?

Make a story

You can take storytelling cues from a variety of places have not been traditionally linked to marketing. They have a lot to tell as far as stories are concerned though. Think—what was the place we went to over centuries to experience strong emotions? We went to the theater. The ancient Greeks had a word for this experience. They called it catharsis: a powerful change in emotions. We can learn a lot from the theater, and this isn't a new concept either. Creating a narrative in a gamified activity is a lot like the theater. What kind of theater can I show you? I want to give you an ad that will captivate you—remember we're talking about engagement—and keep you wide awake for a week. When did you last see an ad that kept you up for a week? I think you know what I'm getting at now.

An ad built from elements of theater. Usually, the participants are free to act out a role and they are having a wonderful time. The engagement from this play is much higher that whatever you could squeeze out of them in a traditional ad. That's basic theater know-how. Nothing revolutionary. The Experience Economy was a book published in 1998 that investigated the shared grounds between work and theater. What can you get from this book? I want you to realize there are two types of recipients of your messages. What are they? First off, a passive recipient. A passive recipient is someone who is flooded with your message but he just doesn't care. The second type on the other hand a recipient who is active and committed to your message.

The difference in engagement between a passive and an active user can be illustrated by watching a sports event on the television and physically being at an arena. You can shout swearwords at the telly as well, but the engagement is just not the same. People who joined the MINI campaign in Stockholm were involved in their experience completely from start to finish. No television ad could have got them to release that kind of energy. Besides the two types of recipients, there are two types of messages you produce.

The first kind of theatre event you create for your customer is repeatable, it's theatre on a stage. If you go to the standard theater house to see the same show twice, assuming no-one falls on the stage with a cardiac arrest, you will see the exact same play. That's also true for cinema and television. If you are watching the same movie for the second time, everything in it stays the same.

The second theater type is improvisational theater. An impromptu message that doesn't repeat. If you take these two types of recipients and the two message types and put them onto a Cartesian coordinate plane, you'll receive four squares that mark different levels of engagement for users. How does this engagement level differ across the squares? Repeated messages result in passive reception in the case of for example television. Television rarely makes you stand up, shout and hoot. Other categories in this square are radio and press. They are essentially shows you put up for your customers. You're offering them up for your customers as a company, but they aren't hugely absorbing.

The quarter in which a recipient is involved and absorbed in an experience, even if the message is repeatable, includes for example a lecture like this one. If I was talking to you in a conference room, if we'd have contact we don't have now since you're watching a video, your engagement would be much higher. I imagine that you're sitting at your desk with a load of other stuff that you are free to do as well. I need to fight for your attention. I'd rather fight for it in a conference room as getting your engagement would be then much easier. Next, there's a passive recipient of improvised content. This is the quarter all video games land onto, as well as social media. If you're on Facebook, all the content you're seeing is improvised. You don't know what's coming at you next. Still, you remain passive.

The highest consumer engagement can be built from a contact with the top right quarter experiences. The consumer is active. He is involved in a wholly improvised experience. Street performance, improv, ARG. Alternative Reality Games allow you to role-play a character. They are held in the urban area, exactly like what you could see in the MINI Stockholm ad. It's theater of sorts. It sets out some you need to complete. You can present your customer with these tasks using a plot and theater. The tasks require varied levels of engagement.

You should acknowledge that the customers of your coffeehouse, store or any other business venture you're running, are liable to engaging in your brand in a myriad of different ways. Some will just click Like on Facebook and that's it. They'll forget about you. But remember that six percent of your customers follow you. Some will subscribe to your newsletter, forward it and collaborate. Some people will turn up at your place if you tell them or ask them to, if you force them or make them curious enough. Others are willing to follow you to an even greater extent. Your task is to prompt people to move from less to more engaged.

To do this, you can fall back on shows and mini-shows that fit into these planes. Your brand, your company fits into the four squares in the same way. Your press ads and television ads are less engaging. If you organize a gig at your bar, people will become more drawn in. Do you see this line? Obviously, there is a customer group that will watch an ad but is less likely to show up at a gig, but in terms of emotional engagement, the group that will remember about you more are the folks that go to your show. The bottom line is being able to offer customers a show or a play in each of the squares.

From a task to a play

How do you move from a task to a play? How do you create gamification step by step? Imagine you're driving your kid in a car. The task you want to complete is straightforward: getting someplace in relative peace and quiet. The kid is four, five or six, and just can't sit in a car for several hours without fidgeting and protesting. You can think of a play to engage your kid: Let's count the passing cars. But this play will soon become boring. There's no goal in sight. We're counting, and counting, and counting… You can however turn this play into a game. For ten red Fords, you'll get an eagle-eye badge. For spotting a car with more than three people in it, a different badge. The more rules there are, the more engaged your kid will be.

Obviously, where there are challenges, there have to be rewards. It's hard to plan for status rewards and making your kid a VIP in such a simple game, but you can manage this is a great way. After your kid gets three eagle-eye badges, he can start looking around for a McDonald's. I guarantee that if you keep your kid occupied with this game, you'll have more peace than if you did nothing or told the kid to simply count the cars.

Another case in point. Losing weight. The task set out for you is to exercise more. The play is counting time and tracking progress. The game, the third level, is to challenge friends just like in Nike+. The last one to run 15 or 30 miles in a week is buying lunch for everyone. You can also put up a show you'll act in. There's an app called Zombies, Run. It's theater you do for yourself. An app that makes you overpower your inner flaws, it's an Ilinx type of game. This app geolocates you (your phone) and the only thing you need to do is to run away from zombies. The more you run, the wider the laps you do round your block, the bigger your base becomes. More people can take safety in it, you get better food rations and so on. When the app sees your running pace is too leisurely or slow, it screeches into your ear, "Run for your live, a zombie is right behind you." The zombies are a virtual but you wouldn't believe how motivating this game is. It's theater you can create yourself.

To recap, what steps can ensure creating good gamification for your company? First off, you need to answer a very basic question: What customer behavior will you encourage? Gamification is a tool you can use. It's not only meant to give your customers a bit of fun from a game. Obviously, this is important as well but gamification is supposed to pay off financially. It's not a marketing fad and needs real business endorsement. What tasks, what behavior patterns do you want to encourage? This is the first and most vital aspect.

Next. Can you think of an epic win that hinges on repeating the behaviors and actions you want to encourage? If you sell coffee, the action you want to encourage is obviously getting your customers back at your coffeehouse to drink coffee. Can you link it to some epic win possibilities? How can you label it? At this point, your narrative begins to take shape.

Next on, you need to map the game to tasks or what we call challenges. See if the reward scheme I told you about is maintained. Are the challenges you develop both long and short-term? Are you rewarding people for effort or for outcome? Remember that it's effort that should be rewarded in the first place. Outcome should be rewarded more sporadically.

The next aspect you should consider is whether you provide all player types with an appealing offer. Remember that different players are motivated with different types of behavior. Some thrive on competition. Other will want to learn as much as they can and share their knowledge with others. Sharing knowledge can be a powerful incentive. The third player category will want to foster social relationships using your game. Do you make it available for them? Can a player interact with other players besides interacting with the game system? Player interaction is often a make or break factor in a project. Have you deployed all the mechanisms I told you about? Does your game involve challenges? Do you have rewards and collections? Does your gameplay hook people? Are the goals you set for your players clear enough? Do they know what they have to do to win?

Players derive little enjoyment from a challenge if they have no way of knowing if they do it the right way. Is your feedback system good enough? Is it clear or ambiguous? You can plan this element but its quality is most apparent in tests.

After that, autonomy. Is there more than one way in which a player can achieve each of your goals? If what you plan for a gameplay is linear, players will feel like they forced down a funnel. They won't like it. Remember, a game is autonomy is achieving mastery. Have you taken care of equipping the game with extra winning options? If I'm your café patron but don't like to drink hectoliters of coffee, is there an alternative way I can win your contest?

A gas station loyalty program. The customer who forks out the most for gas in a month gets a nice prize. For me, this program doesn't really cut it. Why not? I'm not a trucker, I don't have a fleet of cars. It's a program that favors one group of players and is completely unappealing to me. Think about whether or not your customers react the same way. If you have one preferred winning mode, think about whether it shows an unfair preference for one customer group over others. If that's the case, all the other groups will likely opt out of your scheme. They will feel it's not for them.

Do you give your players the instant feedback? I don't mean negative feedback. Let's go back to school for a moment. The instant feedback, school-style, is exactly what you don't want to do. What feedback does a teacher scribble down a checked test? What does it look like? Naturally, you can get a good grade, get full points. But more often than not, the feedback is the mistakes you make. It's very demotivating. Include feedback on progress, on getting toward a goal, not on mistakes. The only direction your player should move is up, and your feedback needs to motivate him to level up.

By way of ending, have you included stages in your game? The worst you can do is to immerse a player in a complicated, multi-rule game environment and tell him to get by on his own. This doesn't work like that. A game should have the following stages. First, training. Video games call it a tutorial. It's a plane in which you can familiarize yourself with the rules of a game. It doesn't have a bearing on later gaming. Next, there's a 'fun' stage where you test and apply the rules you have learnt, again without consequences. Only then come the game proper and fulfilling missions.

The best games overall are the games that merge the tutorial, try-out and goal completion levels seamlessly rather than have them separated. Make your customers immerse in your engagement ladder. If we're speaking of coffeehouses, if a customer walks in and buys a latte, give him a card and say, "Here's a card, if you buy five cups, the sixth one is on us." When he comes back to collect the free coffee, tell him, "You did great! But there's another rule." Remember this? "You're six steps on out of ten to get your own extra-size mug." The more engaged a player becomes, the more rules you can set out for him.

Give him a chance to soak up the experience at his own pace. You can publish a list of tasks on your website, a collection of achievements, and tell your customer, "Choose one and complete it, then choose the next one." Your player needs to have fun completing the tasks because the foremost question you must ask yourself in developing gamification is like I said, "Is it fun?" If it's not, if you yourself can't be bothered to play it freely, if others can't be bothered to start playing because your game is not appealing, doesn't have rewards, the game is just unattractive. If your game is not attractive, go back to square one and start planning it from scratch.

I'll share some gamification ideas that got thrown about in the projects I did. Autonomy. I'm overusing the coffeehouse scenario because it's a handy shorthand I use in lectures. Design your badge on your own. Design your T-shirt on your own. A Café Friend T-shirt is what will advertise your product. If it's something you give to people, great, but it's better to let people design a T-shirt or badge on their own and then get it done for them. Your most frequent and loyal patron will be invited to design Café Friend T-shirt hand-outs for this month. It doesn't cost you anything and the customer satisfaction it can guarantee is amazing.

Bring your friends. Socializers, people who thrive on social interaction, will see this as an inspiration to hang out at your coffeehouse to make friends and foster friendships rather than just drop by to buy a quick cup. Rituals that are fun. I mentioned ordering beer. That wasn't the only ritual, not the only thing we introduced to the restaurant when we gamified it. A product that advertises itself is a different thing. We're working for a Tex-Mex type of joint. Hot dishes, American steaks and so on.

The restaurant has a menu dish that doesn't make any sense—two hottest chili peppers you can think of. They are overpriced at 10 dollars but people keep ordering them. Why?

Because ordering and consumption are made pure fun. When you choose to have the peppers, a loud ding-dong sound goes off. There's a special bell over the bar just for this occasion. Hey, someone has the nerve to try it. Next, a waiter brings a large bucket full of water. Not in a jug, in a bucket. This dish is so hot you will need to down a lot of water. Obviously, not a full bucket, but when the bucket is carried over the entire restaurant, it causes a pleasant uproar, also for other guests who congregate around your table. Then, you get served a nice little plate with two scorching hot peppers, with extra season. You need to gorge down on them, and the entire place is rooting for you. Once you swallow up the peppers, drink from the bucket and survive to hear loud ovations, you can autograph a hall of fame wall. There's a special wall in the restaurant for people who ordered the peppers and ate them. Again it's cost-free for the restaurant, and there's a lot of fun out of it.

That's great gamification. Gamification doesn't need to be about apps, codes, rewards, points. Good gamification allows people to enjoy themselves. That's what you should strive for.

www.ingramcontent.com/pod-product-compliance
Lightning Source LLC
Chambersburg PA
CBHW071239170526
45165CB00003B/1165